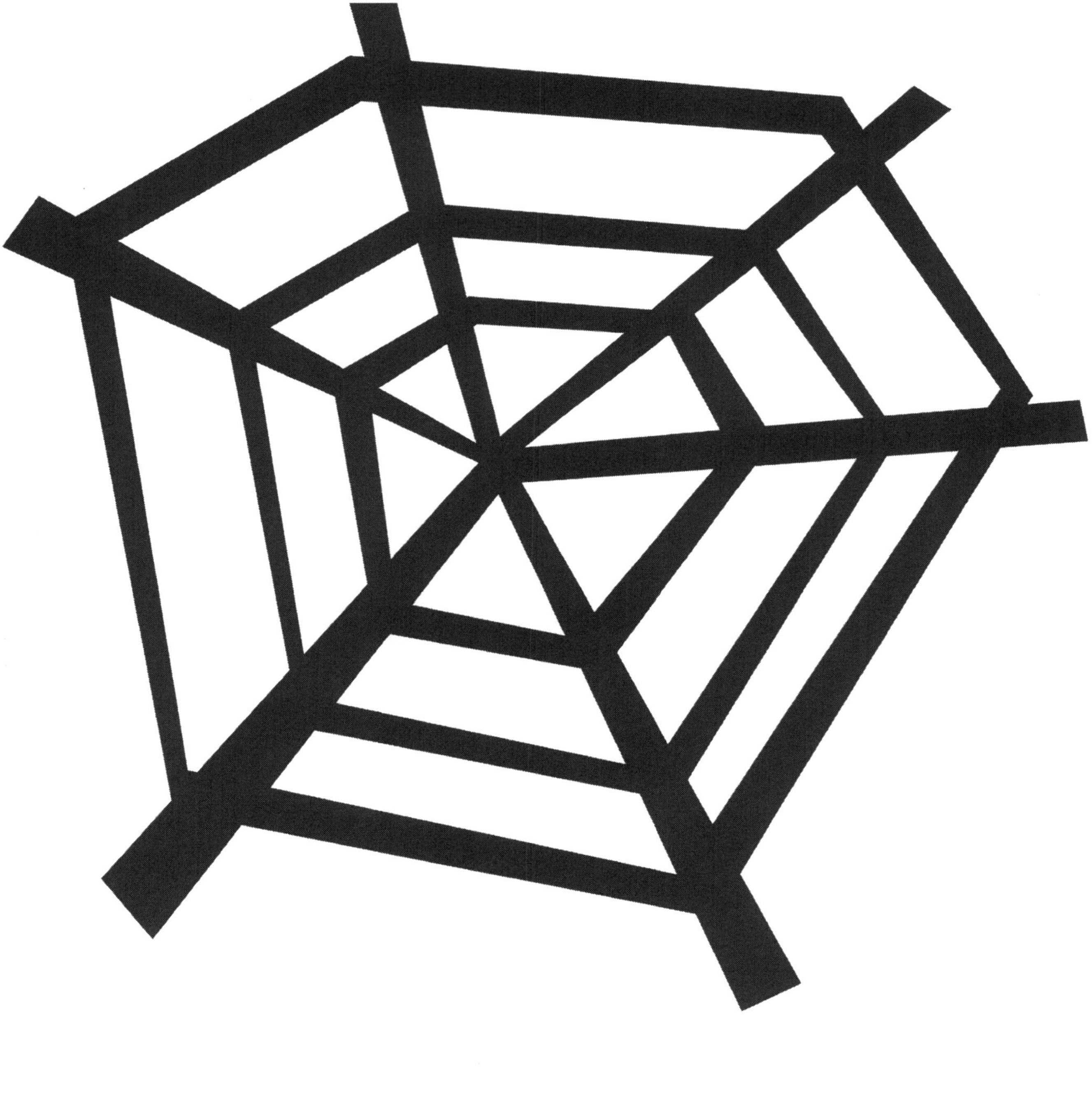

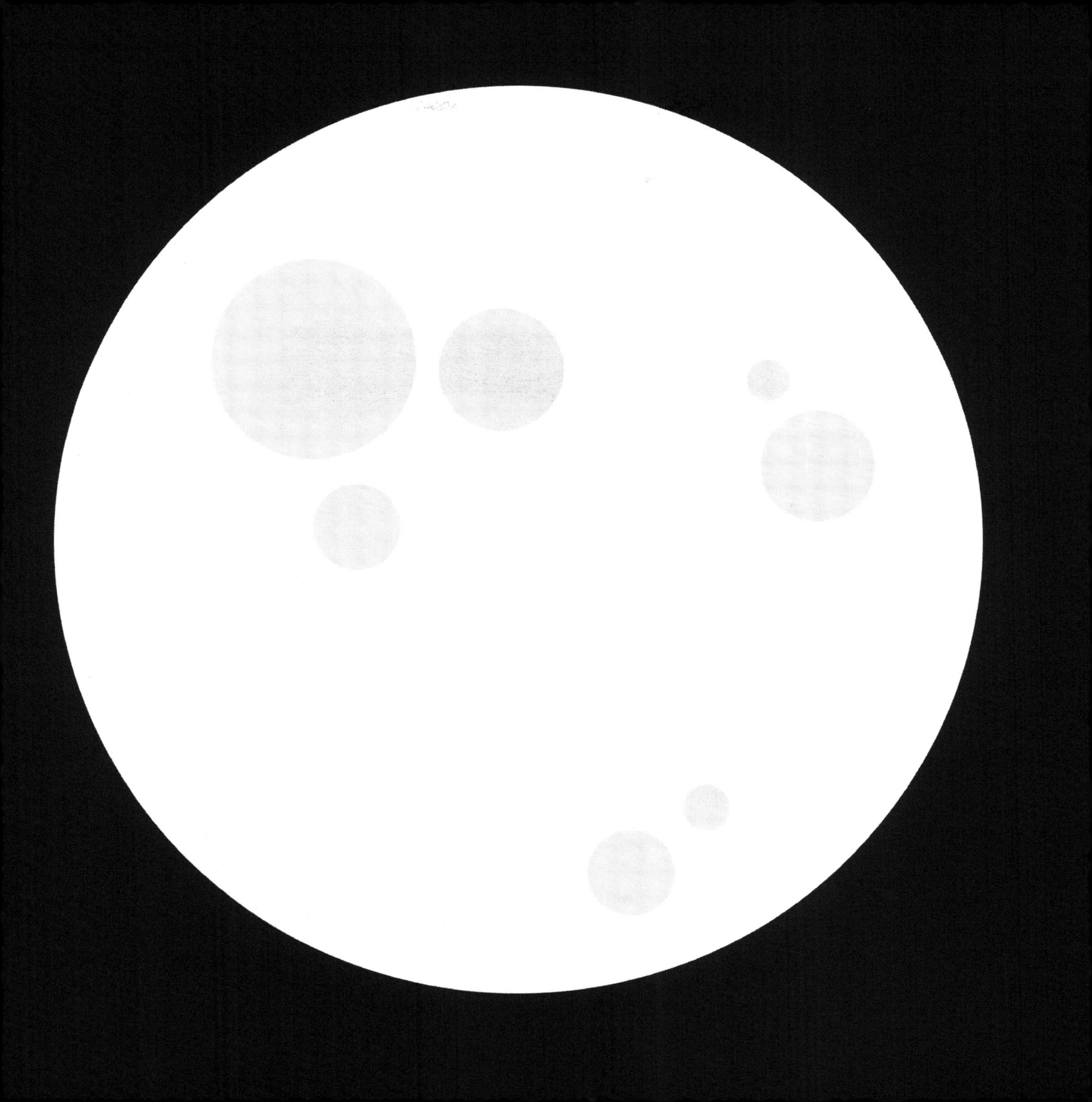

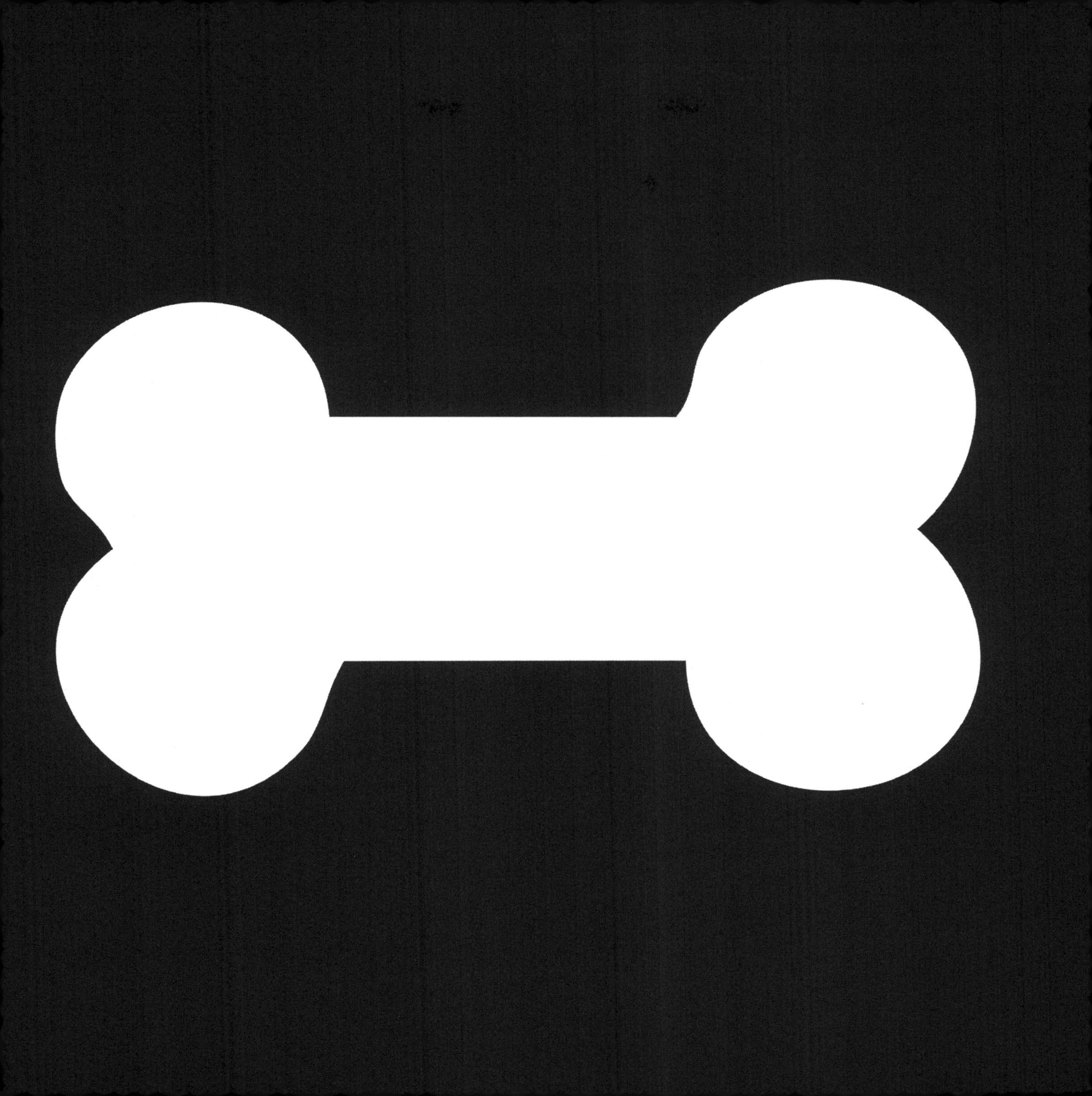

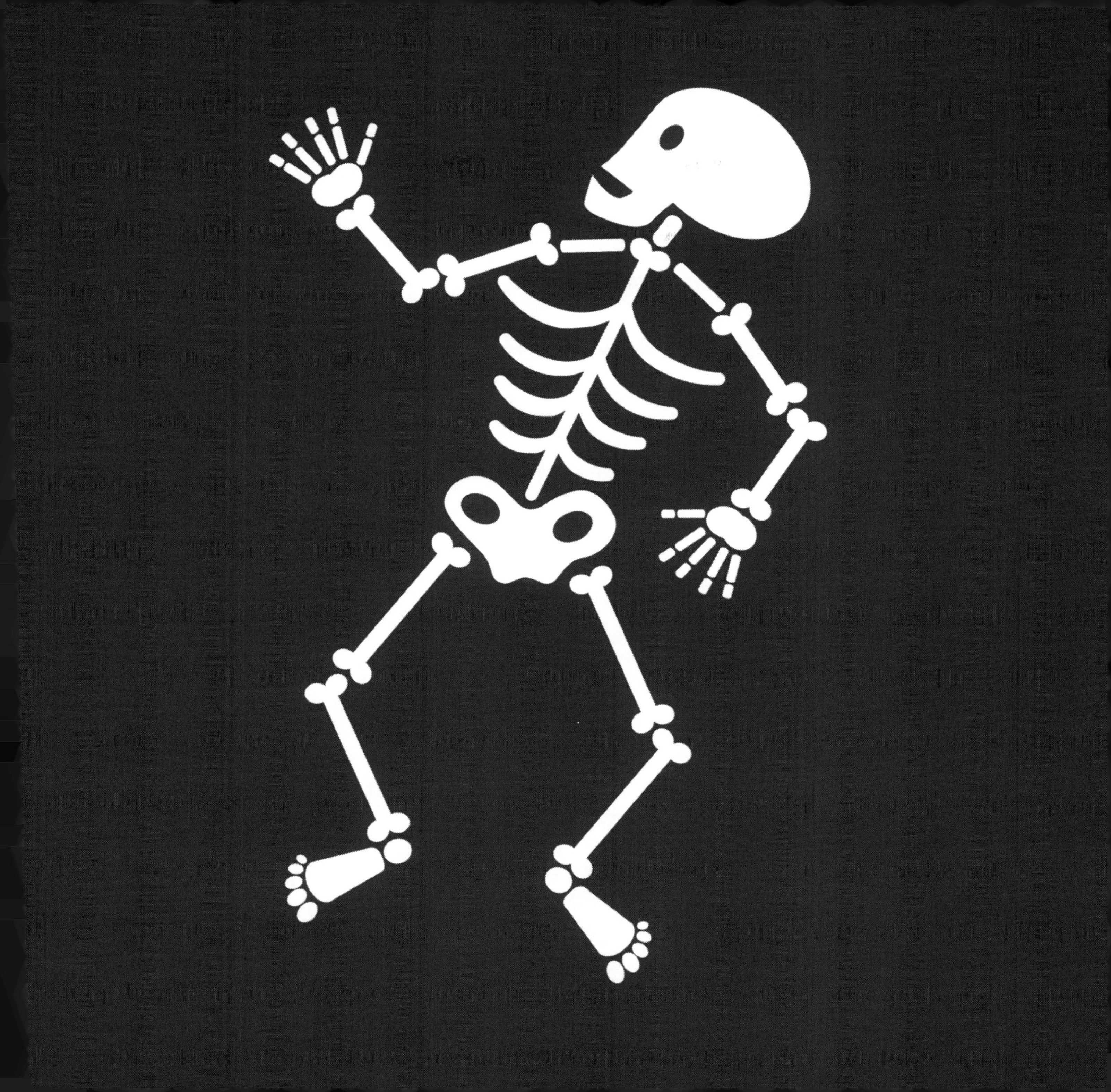

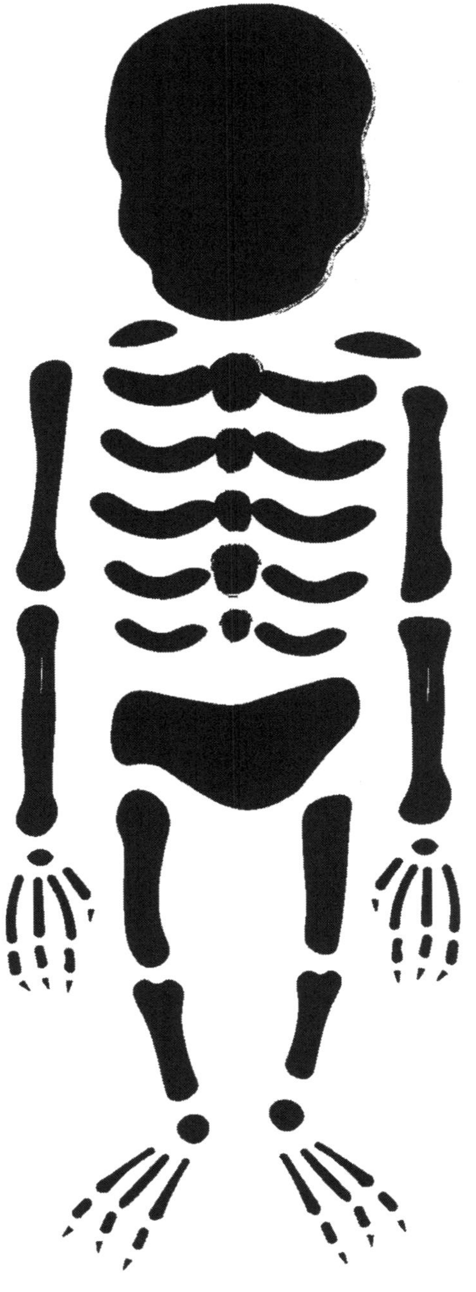

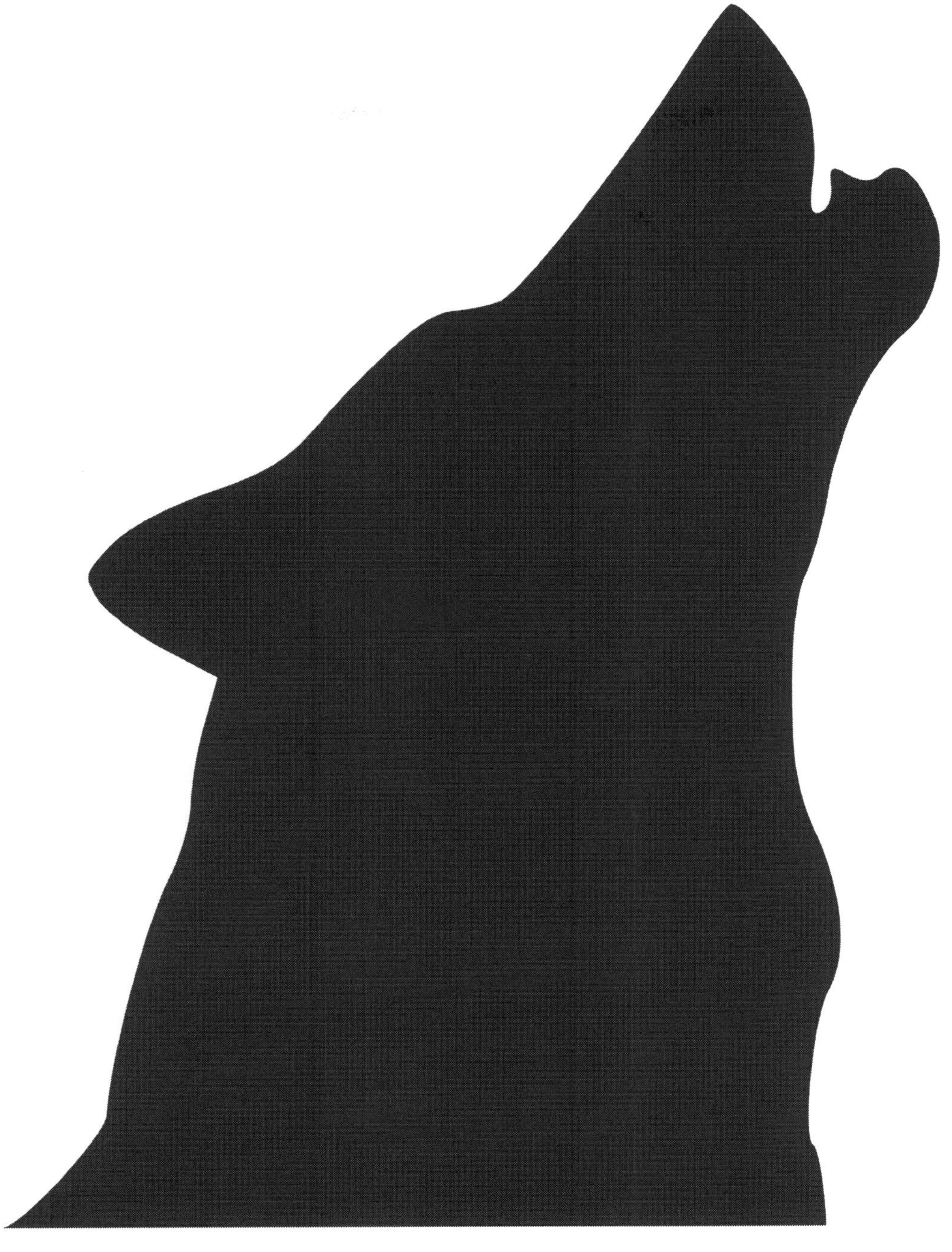

Made in United States
Troutdale, OR
10/03/2024

23377511R00055